Keeping It Off

By Jason L Schembri

This book contains real stories and interviews with my clients. Please note that the personal nature of the content names and identifying information have been changed to protect the privacy of our clients.

The author is not a medical doctor nor in the position of registered authorities to provide you with any kind of professional diagnosis. You should use this information at your own risk. Your life and circumstances may not be suited to the examples provided on these pages.

Published 2022

Print ISBN: 978-1-778-1248-2-2

Ebook ISBN: 978-1-778-1248-1-5

Published by Get You Visible Publishing

www.getyouvisible.com

Contents

With special thanks

To give adequate credit to producing this book, I realize that I have had to dig deeper into all the events and experiences that helped me get back to the beginning.

First and foremost, I want to thank my mother, Lyn, who nurtured my creative side through music and literature from a very young age. My childhood spent reading in libraries sparked my desire to write.

Next, I must thank my father, Alf, whose physical and mental toughness, hard work, and drive laid a foundation for me to be tough, solid, and hardworking.

More recently, I thank the community at www.iamacomeback.com and the founder Mark Jennison (along with coaches Rich and Dave). These men inspired me to step up and become the man I wanted to be. What I learned from them helped me strive to be my best.

To Gerry Robert and Leesa Landry at www.blackcardbooks.com, I give thanks for sharing the perfect structure for book writing with me. I'd have been lost in pages of notes forever without you.

To Mark and Michelle from Ten Degrees Chocolate (and all the staff) who hosted me daily as I toiled away at my chapters for hours. I will never forget your café as my writing home.

To my publishing coach Heather Andrews at www.getyouvisible.com, I am incredibly grateful for your guidance through the final stages of the process. You guided me through the process from manuscript to published book with great expertise.

To my friend Allison Clarke, author of *About a Girl*, who spent hours in the café with me as we both worked on our books, sharing coffee and ideas, and providing support and encouragement.

To the literary knowledge and expertise of the Wild Rose Writer, Mary Lynn Cloghesy at www.marylynncloghesy.com, who took what I believed to be a decent product and helped transform it into something extraordinary.

Last of all, to all my friends and family who have shared my ups and downs (pun intended) and encouraged me through my lived experience in weight management. You've all helped shape this final product in one way or another, and I hope you are proud of this achievement.

Introduction

So here you are. You have just lost weight for the first time, or maybe it's the tenth time. (By rough estimate, my own count was around twenty times.)

Regardless of how you got here, you are likely telling yourself that you will never go back; this time, you really mean it. Not to say that you didn't mean it last time or the time before.

Just the fact that you picked up this book proves you are serious.

You like your new life. You like how you look in the mirror. You like how much energy you have. You can wear all your clothes again finally. You do not want to go back. Ever.

I am here to help you.

One thing that I am not a fitness expert, a weight loss expert, or a dietician. I am "The Weight Management Guy" and am someone like you. This book is not about recipes, good or bad food information, or workout regimes.

I've written this book because I have been where you are and needed the exact help you need today.

I did not want to go back, but I did. Not once or twice, but more than I can count and well into double digits. One could say that I am pretty darn good at losing weight, but I'm an expert at gaining it back. You can guess which one is easier.

To add some context density for you, when I say I was fat, I mean that I was obese. I weighed over 300 pounds. I lived in a mental fog. I could fall asleep anywhere because my metabolism was so slow. If I had to go up more than three stairs (not three flights of stairs, just three steps), I was losing my breath. I could walk but did not believe I could run. In fact, the idea of running was a sad joke. I was depressed and saw no way out. I took my frustration out on those around me, and I could barely look at myself in the mirror. It was hard to confess that my choices led to this horrible, miserable place.

I had spent so much time being unhappy with who I was without really understanding why. Outwardly it was obvious. I was overweight, and while I could always lose weight, I would ultimately gain it back. The frustration and despair of regaining weight may have been more damaging to my mental and emotional health than just remaining overweight.

I finally decided I needed to do something about this. I needed to understand what was behind the constant regaining of weight and find ways to deal with it. The years of research, combined with my trial and error, have resulted in the simple tools in this book.

For many years, I have had a career in executive financial management. Data analysis and research have been my strength for decades. I am so excited to share this with you in the hopes that you can be spared from the years of suffering that I and many others have endured.

Here is your opportunity to keep it off and never go back.

Chapter 1

Just start

We are highly intelligent and reasonable human beings, and yet we have so many challenges beginning activities that contribute to the building of our physical and mental well-being.

We live in a world of convenience where instant gratification can be achieved with little or no effort. In fact, everything we see and hear around us is pushing us towards what is convenient.

Sometimes the goals we want to achieve seem so distant and unachievable. Breaking it down into segments can bring our goals within reach.

Nobody has ever looked back and felt regret at not taking action to achieve something of value. We should always keep this in mind.

Why is it that we keep falling asleep and "forgetting" what we want to achieve?

I use an alarm to wake me up every day (or I'd sleep a long time!), so why not set alarms for ourselves for other things too?

Something woke us up when we decided to lose weight, improve our fitness, and get in shape. Something gave us the desire or the sense of urgency to act.

If we are serious about our success, we should set up a framework to help us succeed. We do this in our business lives, so why not for our health and wellbeing? That's why we must "just start."

Nobody has ever looked back and felt regret at not taking action to achieve something of value. We should always keep this in mind.

Why do we spend so much time in our heads?

We trust our brain because it's us, but our brain is often very unkind to us and not always working for our true benefit.

All the time spent in our heads is a time of zero action. Our brain works quickly with the intention of making a decision, so we can actually DO something.

Unfortunately, when we talk to ourselves, we are likely not learning anything new.

How much of our day is spent in our own heads?

We have about 16 hours a day available to do something. How much of this time needs to be spent thinking as opposed to acting?

When we wake up in the morning, we have achieved zero at that moment in time. Who wants to go to bed that same evening without having contributed anything of value to their life or their success?

With all this time in a day available for us to get what we want, surely we can easily carve out the time we need to move forward. We did this to lose weight, so now we just need to adjust to something new and sustainable to protect the work we've done and live our best lives.

How can we find the connection between the GOOD thoughts we have and turning them into actions?

Remember I said *good* thoughts. Just like a brainstorming session in a work meeting, we are not going to have great ideas with every thought we have. Identifying *good* thoughts is important before we can move to the appropriate actions.

Sadly, our good intentions do not magically turn into action just because we want them to. Turning our learning into action is too important to just leave to chance.

We can be so in love with the idea of doing something great. We fantasize about the great things we can and will do. If we never take the step from thought into action, we inevitably feel regret, frustration, and anger that can spill over into our lives and harm ourselves and our relationships.

The failure to turn thoughts into actions is likely a major contributing factor to why you are here. Let's deal with this together.

What is the value to us of learning something but never applying it in our lives?

A great real-life example is the story of my friend Bryan, who loves to dance. He takes dance lessons regularly to improve his skills and goes dancing whenever possible. Every time I see him after an evening out dancing, he is so alive and joyful. To imagine Bryan never using the skills, he's acquired makes me sad. The lesson here is clear. It's the application of what we learn that brings us true satisfaction, not the acquiring of the skill.

Every time we learn something and don't apply it, we have wasted our time. It's true that we can't apply all that we are exposed to or don't have the need for all that we experience. The things we decide we want to learn, because we have the intention of applying them in our lives, need our focus if we want to follow through.

Sadly, our good intentions do not magically turn into action just because we want them to. Turning our learning into action is too important to just leave to chance.

If we hate procrastination so much, why are we so intent on becoming experts at it?

Every time we procrastinate, we make a choice. The choice, unfortunately, is often to postpone something we truly want and put something less valuable first. I consider this the greatest disservice we can do to ourselves.

If only we could find a way to know what things are most important to us *and* give those things priority. I am going to show you how to do this.

I see my procrastination as an enemy who wants me to fail. Taking this saboteur's power away was the key to my success in my weight management, but even more so in paving my way to creating the life I've always wanted.

How did I learn to Just Start?

In 2001, I was preparing to take the CMA (Certified Management Accountant) National Entrance exam. Statistically, only half of the candidates writing the exam were expected to pass. I was scared! My study group hired a CMA Mentor named Bob Garries to help guide us through the exam process and give us feedback to help us prepare. After writing a few practice exams, Bob took me aside and gave me the advice that would change my life. He said, "Jason, you just need to start writing." That was it. Bob had analyzed my behaviour and concluded that my biggest problem was *not* starting.

When it came time to write the exam, less than a week later, Bob's words reverberated loudly in my mind. I just started writing. In the three hours of the exam, I wrote thirty pages. I can barely remember what I wrote as I was so focused on taking action. I had gotten out of my head. I passed with a very respectable score. The national average pass rate for that year was 51%, so in other words, every other person failed.

While "Just Start" is a key tool for your success, it is still only the beginning.

"Just Start" has enabled me to begin a successful weight loss journey again, and again, and again, but knowing what to do is not the same as doing it. It was to be almost ten years before I found the tool that enabled me to escape that cycle.

What is the five-second rule?

Any valuable tool should be simple. That does not mean it will be easy, but it does need to be simple.

If a tool is not simple, we just won't use it. We need to understand it, and it must resonate with us.

In November 2020, the book "The Five Second Rule" by Mel Robbins was recommended to me. Like myself, Mel was frozen in the world of inaction, and it was preventing success in her life. Mel's revelation is detailed and deep, and I would highly recommend her book to further understand the science and success behind this simple concept.

"If you have an impulse to act on a goal, you must physically move within five seconds, or your brain will kill the idea." – Mel Robbins

To summarize Mel's concept, I will state this as simply as I can.

When you feel the thought, idea, or urge to do something, count out loud from five down to one and then move. If you do not act within these five seconds, your brain will eliminate the motivation to act, and you will literally do nothing.

At the end of this countdown, if you were lying down, you might sit up; if you were sitting down, you could stand up; if

*While "Just Start"
is a key tool for
your success, it is
still only the
beginning.*

you were standing, you would start walking; if you were walking, you might start running. The goal is that you will physically move towards an action that will propel you to achieve something that your own brain has just told you that you need to achieve.

This is how we will turn what we think into what we do, turn thoughts into actions, learning into application, and most importantly, vanquish our procrastination.

Procrastination is the art of thinking of doing something and then doing nothing. When you think of it this way, does it take much skill or effort to be a master of this? Procrastination is the easiest of skills to learn because it involves no work, no research, no study, just inaction. Guess where this leads? Nowhere.

ACTION ITEM FOR THIS CHAPTER:

Find your best tools to help you to "Just Start" something.

Over the next few chapters, I am going to help you uncover an abundance of actions that you will be motivated to "Just Start," so don't feel bad if nothing of consequence is coming to mind right now. Perhaps "Just Start" with something simple for the time being.

Any valuable tool should be simple. That does not mean it will be easy, but it does need to be simple.

Chapter 2

Eliminating root causes

Can the strategies we used to lose weight help us keep that weight off, or do we need something new?

Our weight loss journey was likely very focused on that one thing without much insight into life beyond. What got us here is not likely going to help keep us here.

Every diet has something in common. They all have an end date. Once we have achieved the desired weight loss, we are finished, and in most cases, the tenets and rules of the diet abandon us, or we abandon them. At the very least, we must make some lifestyle changes as we embark on a program of maintenance because this is a new challenge that will likely require new goals and strategies.

Because many diets require a lifestyle of restriction and deprivation (perhaps that sounds a little dramatic, but that's how I saw it during my multiple weight loss journeys), it's not so easy to adopt a modified version because we may feel resentment towards the diet that got us here. We not only need something new but also need something sustainable that allows us to enjoy our life to the fullest.

If we don't identify the root causes behind our weight gain, we are doomed to repeat the cycle over and over.

How do we determine why we do what we do or what we did?

We know we gained weight. That much was obvious when we put on our clothes, looked in the mirror, stepped on the scale, or climbed the stairs, but we've already identified and fixed the external problem.

If we don't identify the root causes behind our weight gain, we are doomed to repeat the cycle over and over.

Perhaps this is your first gain and loss, and if so, be thankful that you may never have to deal with this again. If you are like me, you may have dealt with this more times than you can count. Personally, I feel like I'm an expert at weight loss and can confidently begin a weight loss regime knowing that I will succeed. Thankfully, once I dealt with the root causes, I never had to go back to being overweight again.

Most of us have been in a job interview where we were asked what our weaknesses were. The potential employer wants to know what challenges we've encountered, but more importantly, they want to know what we've done to deal with these weaknesses. An example I've heard many times - though not necessarily a weakness - is that a candidate may say that they work too hard. One way they may be mitigating this is to take a time management workshop or try to organize their work-life balance more intentionally. Should we not also be doing this in our personal lives? Eliminating or mitigating our weaknesses is a key factor in our future success and happiness.

Are we able to trace our lives back to the point where we got stuck?

The thing about trauma is that it's not our fault, yet we still must deal with it. Something was inflicted upon us that changed our lives, and if left unaddressed, it could continue to cause us harm. While we've addressed the physical symptoms, mostly through diet and exercise, the underlying causes behind any weight gain may still need to be tackled.

I recognize that trauma is no simple thing, and I am definitely not an expert in dealing with it. I do recognize the need for professional help, advice, and support when addressing this, and so I defer to the professionals in this area, of which there are many. Choose wisely.

What were my root causes, and how did I deal with them?

I am grateful that I do not have a history of serious trauma; however, I discovered that my issues related to guilt and shame and the damage this caused to my sense of self-worth. If you don't feel worthy of success, then you will not succeed. It really was quite simple that once I had identified the events in my life that led to this, I was able to mentally walk (and talk) my way through each one and resolve them. As I dealt with each issue, I could feel my sense of self-worth increase which ultimately restored my confidence and my will to succeed. If you can recognize that you are valuable regardless of what others think, you can develop great respect and love for yourself. We do not have a natural tendency to harm what we love and respect.

Is there such a thing as an addictive nature, and if so, does this doom me to failure?

This is a great topic for debate and could likely be argued one way or the other with success, as there are many valid points to be made on either side. The conclusions that you could draw could be easily defended regardless of the side you chose. One could argue that "it's in my nature" or "my actions are totally my choice." Either way, we can make either perspective work to our benefit.

Let's assume we've decided that we have an addictive nature and are doomed to be susceptible to addiction. Let's make this work in our favour. We do have a choice over WHAT we will be addicted to. Let's agree that we are likely going to be addicted to something that we perceive will bring us pleasure and choose the things that make us feel good. Right now, go ahead and make a list of everything that makes you feel great, regardless of whether it's healthy or not. Now, highlight everything on the list that is going to make you truly happy. Does this list excite you? Do the same by highlighting the things that won't make you truly happy. I bet you're seeing some clear distinctions between the two groups. Can you choose to be addicted to the truly good things? Would that make you happy? You are right; it will.

Now let's assume that we do not have an addictive nature and that everything is our own choice and within our own capacity to choose. We can look at that same list and simply choose those truly good items to occupy our time and effort. Regardless of which side of the fence you are on, it still comes down to us choosing the things you truly love and desire and taking appropriate steps to pursue them.

What is candida yeast and how does it impact weight management?

The Oxford dictionary defines candida as "a yeastlike parasitic fungus that can sometimes cause thrush." This is a massive understatement, and the reality is that this is like saying, "Falling off a fifty-story building can sometimes cause mild bruising." Candida is of much higher consequence and concern to our health and can be a MAJOR factor in weight gain and a barrier to losing weight. Of course, this also means it is a big impediment to maintaining a healthy weight. Thankfully, there are many resources and tools available to combat candida. Candida lives inside us and constantly causes us to crave sugar and starches. Our own appetite is hijacked to feed this unwelcome house guest.

To get a good understanding of candida, I recommend the book Candida Secrets by Cynthia Perkins, M.Ed.

I needed to deal with a candida yeast overgrowth issue, and if you've lost weight, then you have likely dealt with this already, even if you were not aware of it at the time. There are many cleanses available to help with this issue that you can purchase off the shelf of any good health supplement store. A good candida cleanse will include a broad range of natural antifungals to kill the candida yeast, combined with a low sugar and low starch diet that will starve the candida while you're killing it.

The elimination of candida yeast overgrowth is going to make your weight management goals and lifestyle much easier. Without addressing this, you will constantly be fighting your own body when it comes to cravings.

Why do we tend to stand in judgment over everyone, including ourselves?

If there was ever a greater waste of time or a more significant cause of pain, it would be judgment. Let's break it down into two main categories so we can more effectively deal with it: judgment of others and judgment of ourselves.

When we judge others, there are usually no consequences for those we have judged. In fact, those we find guilty (and it's almost always guilty) are often oblivious to the fact that they have been on trial. There is no sentence to be carried out on the guilty. Instead, we carry this guilt on behalf of the person we judged. We need to let it go. Let people have their problems.

If there was ever a greater waste of time or a more significant cause of pain, it would be judgment.

When we judge ourselves, we are in a position to give ourselves consequences. If we stopped to think about this, we would realize that someone else is always willing to judge us, and so we don't really need to make the effort of self-judgment. Don't we always find ourselves guilty? What horrible defense attorneys we are! Our biggest judgment is that we are unworthy of success and therefore doomed to failure. Because we can inflict consequences on ourselves, you can bet that we will fail when we judge ourselves. Let's not make this a barrier to our own success.

Can we forgive ourselves and others?

Forgiveness goes hand in hand with judgment. There is nobody to forgive if no one is guilty.

When somebody hurts us, we might have a hard time forgiving them. I believe the main reason for this is because we don't truly understand what forgiveness is. Forgiveness is for your own well-being, not for the well-being of the person that caused you harm. Forgiveness is not about telling you that what happened is okay but about saying that you are not going to carry the pain and burden of what someone did to you. The Christian meaning of forgiving is about being "for" (or in favour of) "giving" (or handing over) the judgment to God. This frees you from any burden without excusing someone's bad behaviour.

Withholding forgiveness is like drinking poison and waiting for the other person to die. You've judged them guilty, yet you are going to bear the pain while they are completely oblivious to any consequences. So, I say to you, forgive quickly and sincerely for your health. Retaining the burden creates physical barriers to your health.

Forgiveness is for your own well-being, not for the well-being of the person that caused you harm.

What's one easy tool to help deal with unresolved conflict?

A few years ago, while working in a financial executive role, I was contemplating strategies that I could use to reduce barriers between myself and my team members to build more trust and better personal relationships. I came up with an idea that I thought might work and tried it out on one of my colleagues.

I held weekly one-on-one meetings with each team member and decided to add a small change. I began with Brent. I chose Brent because we already had a strong relationship, and we shared common ideals. I felt it would be more comfortable to pilot this with him.

I told Brent that I wanted to try out something new and shared the premise behind it. Despite some uncertainty, he agreed to try it. Here's how our first conversation went:

Me: *"Brent, what is the most uncomfortable issue between you and me that we can talk about and try to resolve right now?"*

This question was followed by a slightly uncomfortable silence as Brent considered the question and searched his memory (and feelings, I suspect) to come up with the answer. In hindsight, I know he was also deciding if he felt safe enough in our relationship to bring up something that would likely be challenging. After we allowed some moments to pass, Brent finally had something to share.

Brent: *"In a team meeting a few months ago, I shared an idea with the team, and I felt like you dismissed the idea prematurely. I felt disrespected, and I guess I still feel that this is an issue for me and between us."*

I could see that Brent was looking at me to see how I would react to him bringing this up with me. Was he safe? Was I going to react positively or negatively? As this was a test, I also had to search within myself to think about how I felt about this.

Me: *"Brent, thank you for sharing this. I had no idea I had dismissed your idea and made you feel this way. I apologize and will try to be more thoughtful in the future. Can we talk about your idea now?"*

Brent then laughed and showed visible signs of relief. His risk of sharing his feelings with me had been successful because I accepted his concerns and reacted in a way that made him feel safe and secure.

Brent: *"Actually, after the meeting, I worked on the idea some more and determined it wasn't going to work, so there's no harm done. Thanks for asking me to bring this up. I feel really good now."*

I felt the same way as Brent, and I realized that what we were doing was being very deliberate about addressing issues that might otherwise remain buried. I had just created a formal tool for recognizing and dealing with conflict.

In future meetings with Brent, we each took turns bringing up whatever was the most uncomfortable thing between us. We both found it amusing to work our way through the "list" of issues. The items became so trivial that we often laughed as we discussed them.

Not only did our relationship become stronger and more trusting, but we also became more attuned to identifying any new issues before they could become conflicts, as we were now in the habit of detecting and addressing interpersonal conflict on a regular basis. It had become part of who we were and how we behaved.

I began to introduce this tool into my personal life as well with the same success. Once the initial discomfort had been overcome by tackling this for the first time with someone, it became easier and easier to do until it was something that both people were comfortable with.

One example of how I employed this in my personal life was in reference to my relationship with my mother. As a child, I don't recall receiving much physical affection from my mother, and I decided to "challenge" her about this. It was clear that the topic was very uncomfortable for her, as it was for me, but I was persistent, and we worked our way through it. I found that she had grown up in a very formal family structure where there was little affection shown to the children, and she carried this forward to her own family. By the end of the conversation, we agreed that we could be more affectionate toward each other and enjoyed a much closer relationship which included more words of sentiment and feelings on a more frequent basis. I realized that embracing and resolving uncomfortable conversations can often be as beneficial for the other person as it is for me.

ACTION ITEM FOR THIS CHAPTER:

Find your way to recognize the root causes in your life and then find the best way to deal with them.

Forgive someone.

Identify any unresolved conflict you might be holding onto with someone and ask permission to start an uncomfortable conversation with them.

Embracing and resolving uncomfortable conversations can often be as beneficial for the other person as it is for me.

If we can work out what we want and why then we can begin to build a plan to achieve it.

Chapter 3

What would you do if you knew you couldn't fail?

Are you pursuing your dreams?

Here's one thing I can safely say is true. It was never your dream, or mine, to gain weight than to have to spend time losing it. So, why would we spend time on something we *don't* want when there's something out there we really *do* want?

Everybody has some dream they want to fulfill, some goal they want to achieve.

If we can work out what we want and why then we can begin to build a plan to achieve it.

When we can figure out what we want in life and focus our energy on pursuing it, we are not going to spend time cultivating bad habits that cause us to gain weight. A purpose-driven life is filled with energy and passion.

Are you passionate about what you are doing every day?

Let's make a list of all the things were are doing in our life currently. (This list is private, so you can be completely honest with yourself.) Highlight all the things you do that create energy and excitement in your life; hopefully, there will be many. Losing weight may be on this list, but the work of losing weight may not be something that made you feel good; rather, it was the result that did.

These highlighted items on your list are going to be your key indicators in working out what your true dreams are. If you are already pursuing your dreams, then you have a great head start. I had to start from scratch, and if you are too, that's okay. We are all starting from different places.

The last part of this exercise is to write down the things you always wanted to do but never did. The information from the first list should feed this exercise. Maybe you have one thing, and maybe you have ten. Try to limit yourself to no more than ten so that it will be easier to focus.

Can you envision your dreams without any limits or barriers?

We have a natural tendency to place limits on ourselves. We think about our current resources like time, money, knowledge, and more, and we begin to create limits that restrict our ability to think and dream, to our maximum potential.

In his 1973 book, titled "You Can Become the Person You Want to Be," author Robert Schuller asked the question, "What goals would you set for yourself if you knew you couldn't fail?"

Was there ever a more freedom-inspiring statement? With this in mind, rewrite your dream without any limits. Imagine that you are going to be successful. It's your dream, so why shouldn't you succeed?

We have a natural tendency to place limits on ourselves.

Have you ever thought that you could achieve more than you think you can?

We are astounded when we hear stories of people overcoming incredible adversity to achieve their lofty goals. We can hear these people addressing us at conferences as keynote speakers and are suitably impressed and inspired. Nothing is stopping us from being just like these people and reaching goals that we think are beyond our reach.

For those of us that have lost weight, the analogy of running a race is one that we can relate to when it comes to setting and achieving a goal. After losing weight (or during the process), we begin to realize that running may be possible once again, or perhaps for the first time ever. The goal I had set for myself during my weight loss journey was to run a half-marathon mountain race. At the time, it seemed extreme, and I was worried I couldn't achieve it. Little did I know that a few years later, after completing several half-marathons, I would skip full marathons entirely and complete 50km+ ultra-marathons. Each time I stepped up to something more challenging, I noticed that I was capable of much more than I thought. This does not need to happen in hindsight only.

Have you written your best story? Achieved your highest goals? Review the list again, and don't hold back! Would it be so bad to set a goal to run an ultra-marathon (50+ kilometres), then end up running a "regular" marathon (42.2 kilometres)? Did you know that less than 1% of the world's population has run a marathon? Would you feel like you failed if you set a goal of running an ultra-marathon but had to settle for only being in the top 1% of runners on the planet? One thing I can guarantee you is that if you only set a goal of running a 5km race, that's all you will achieve. You will always wonder if you could have achieved more. Don't be afraid to dream big, plan for success, then do it. The feeling of achievement you can experience will drive you forward in all areas of your life.

Every time we are
held back by fear,
we are postponing a
positive step
forward in our lives.

How can we overcome our fear?

Fear is a very powerful emotion, and it has an impact on us. It can stop us from taking action. Every time we are held back by fear, we are postponing a positive step forward in our lives. I don't know anyone who felt regret in overcoming their fear. So, if we know this, then why do we still give it so much power?

We can't eradicate fear from our lives, but we can have courage. We show courage when we feel fear but take action anyway.

How can we build our courage to the extent that it is more powerful than our fear?

The process is simple. When we feel fear, rather than focusing on that emotion, we need to think about all the positive emotions we will feel if we overcome fear by taking action. This creates an emotional battle between our fear and our positive emotions. The more positive emotions we can muster, the stronger the likelihood that the battle will turn to our side. Think about some examples of powerful positive emotions like joy, excitement, love, peace, confidence, and pride. The list is much longer, but if we can stack a few positive emotions against the negative emotion of fear, we are on track to overcome it.

Logic is the other aspect that can help us. If we analyze the source of our fear, breaking it down into data and facts, we can see where the fear is coming from. All we need to do is play the scenario through until we find that the fear is an accumulation of all the negative outcomes we can conceive of, most of which will never happen. We spend too much time worrying about things that will never come to pass. Our own experiences confirm this to be true.

Can our passions and dreams become more compelling than our distractions?

In 2011, I knew what my dream was, but for ten years, I did nothing about it. I had articulated it, recorded it, and made notes about it, nothing more. My dream just sat there for ten years in the back of my mind while I moved through life doing other things that may have given me some satisfaction, but I knew deep down I was missing my calling. My dream was to write this book to help others succeed.

When we know what our dream is and decide we want to pursue it, we need to generate a passion and excitement about our dream that is more compelling than any distractions. It needs to be a top priority. I'm not saying it should supersede career, family, or health, but it should be more important than trivial things like entertainment.

The moment we decide that something is important to us and make a plan to achieve it, we can progress quickly, and that feels good.

The challenge is to make it a part of our daily lives. More on how to do this is in the next chapter (Building Your Habits).

ACTION ITEM FOR THIS CHAPTER:

Identify your dreams without boundaries, make them bigger than we believe possible, and get excited about them. This is what will drive your goals and actions, and success.

Write a single paragraph on how you would feel if you were living your dreams right now. Think about the emotions you feel when you read this paragraph back to yourself.

At the end of a weight loss journey, we are at a crossroads because we no longer need the habit that caused us to lose weight. We need a new strategy.

Chapter 4

Building your habits

There are many definitions of what a habit is. Here is the one I like the best: "An acquired pattern of behavior that has become almost involuntary as a result of frequent repetition." Regardless of the definition we like, we can agree on a few things when it comes to habits:

1) they can be good or bad
2) It takes repetition to build a habit
3) We can create or eliminate a habit with awareness and action.

As I ended each of my weight loss journeys, I recognized two things when it came to habits:

1) I had interrupted some bad habits that caused me to gain weight.
2) I had developed some new habits that caused me to lose weight.

At the end of a weight loss journey, we are at a crossroads because we no longer need the habit that caused us to lose weight. We need a new strategy. However, the old habits that caused us to gain weight may still be lurking in the shadows waiting to reinstate themselves into our lives. I call these old habits "dead horses," and there is no value in going back to them as they won't be taking us anywhere.

This is a vulnerable time, so we need to make sure that we plan sufficiently so we are ready to adopt new habits that take us forward to a stable and happy future.

If you've followed through so far from chapter one, you now know how to "Just Start", how to eliminate your root causes, and how to identify what your dream is. With this in mind, we can now build the habits that will drive your success every day without any concern about regaining the weight you fought so hard to lose.

What is the difference between motivation and discipline?

It's important to understand two keywords when it comes to building habits: motivation and discipline. Knowing what they are and how to use them is the key to our success. Motivation is what drives us to do something and ties strongly to our emotions and our feelings. Because of this, motivation can change frequently and dramatically, making it very inconsistent and an unstable method to rely upon. Discipline, on the other hand, involves commitment and accountability which makes it a much stronger support for our success. When we have discipline, it may be derived from our motivation, but it is very stable and does not change according to our emotions and feelings.

It only takes a moment of motivation to make a plan and start building a habit. Adding discipline to this motivation is what we are going to rely upon to build that habit, ensuring we achieve the goal that motivated us. We need both motivation and discipline to succeed. They are perfect partners.

Why it's important to start small.

While it is the good habits we build through discipline that will become the strongest drivers of our long-term success, we need to keep refreshing our motivation to enjoy the journey. If our goal was to lose 100 pounds within two years (as I did), wouldn't it be miserable if we hated 729 days of this journey and only loved the final day of 730, assuming we had achieved our goal? We need to feel the joy to recharge and refresh our motivation so that we can keep our minds on what we aim to achieve.

Producing dopamine in our bodies is a great way to spark motivation because dopamine creates a positive feedback loop, along with feelings of pleasure and satisfaction. While the list of things we can do to produce dopamine is endless, I'll list a few of my favourites here that motivate and keep me on the right track in no particular order:

- **Sexual Intimacy (within the confines of your own boundaries, ideals, and moral compass)**
- **Exercising**
- **Playing games**
- **Hugging (friends, family, pets)**
- **Completing a task (I make many tasks each day so I can complete more)**
- **Losing weight (obviously)**
- **Being creative (music, art, writing)**
- **Listening to music**
- **Meditating (including prayer)**
- **Getting some sun**
- **Receiving a massage (one of my favourites)**
- **Eating a healthy diet**
- **Consuming caffeine (another favourite)**

While our lives are made up of the ongoing pursuit of goals, if we step back, we can see that arriving at each destination was a very small part of our lives. The largest blocks of time in our lives are spent taking the journey between goals. If we want to be truly happy, we should learn to be present and aware and to appreciate our time, our challenges, and our successes. Time is one resource we cannot get more of, so we should treat it with respect.

How can we make a habit out of something we don't perceive to be enjoyable?

There are many habits that we build in our lives that we don't perceive to be fun, but we build them nonetheless because we know they are beneficial. They include things like cleaning our homes, washing our dishes, getting up for work, and brushing our teeth (I'd include flossing, but that habit still feels beyond reach to me). At some point, we either decided these things were important, or someone helped us to understand that they were important. Either way, as adults, we do these things without much fuss. Right now, we are in a great position to begin building new habits that we can agree will be beneficial to us, but perhaps we don't feel like we will enjoy them initially. Let's explore some ways to successfully build these habits.

We can explore habit pairing. We likely already have many habits that we enjoy and perform on a regular basis. We can build a new habit by "piggybacking" it onto an existing habit that we already have. I began this process by listing all the habits I currently have, the good and the bad. (I set aside the bad ones to consider how to eliminate these later.) Next, I highlighted the ones that I really enjoy and considered which ones I could logically match up with building a new habit.

Here is an example: I love coffee. I drink multiple cups per day. It is a habit that I have had for a long time and one that I thoroughly enjoy. I wanted to build a habit of writing this book every morning but found that I was having difficulty doing this on a regular basis. Some days I felt motivated, but on others, I did not. I decided to make the following commitment to myself:

We can build a new habit by "piggybacking" it onto an existing habit that we already have.

I would not begin drinking my first coffee of the day until I was sitting at my desk and writing my book. Because I love my coffee and I am in the habit of drinking my first cup at the beginning of the day, I created the motivation to write, which very quickly developed into a discipline that has now become a habit. I also noticed that because I loved drinking coffee, I slowly began to love writing my book. I had to "Just Start".

I invite you to try this same exercise and list all of your current habits, focussing on all of your good habits and considering which ones would pair well with the building of a new habit.

How can I go deeper in building my habits?

When it comes to understanding how or why to build habits, I refer to my favourite author on this topic, James Clear, and his best-selling book Atomic Habits.

In James's book, he impresses upon the reader that the concept of setting goals, while important, is much less important than focusing on the system you employ to bring about building a habit (or the elimination of an unwanted habit).

James highlights four "laws" in his book that can be employed to bring about better habits. They are:

1) **Make it obvious**
2) **Make it attractive**
3) **Make it easy**
4) **Make it satisfying**

One other element of James's book that impressed me was the concept of making oneself one percent better each day. This aligns well with the notion of generating dopamine.

Why is the story of the 100 push-ups a great example of a small but cumulative improvement?

My cousin Phil runs Shindo Karate in my home city of Melbourne, Australia. One Christmas, when I was visiting, Phil said he was concerned about his karate students losing focus over the Christmas break, so he had decided to give his students homework to keep them fit. I was intrigued.

The basic concept is that they needed to build up to 100 push-ups every day. Phil gave them some simple rules to follow:

1) The first set of push-ups each day must be the maximum number of push-ups you can do
2) The first set should be, at a minimum, as many as the first set from the previous day
3) By the end of the Christmas break, the goal was to complete all 100 push-ups in one single set

This last part I perceived as daunting, and I could see how it would be quite the achievement if one should make it to that final goal.

Upon returning home to Canada, I decided to incorporate this challenge into my daily routine. I could perceive many benefits to this health regime, and hindsight has confirmed this:

1) I slowly built a very healthy daily habit
2) I felt challenged every day
3) I produced dopamine every morning
4) I felt the desire to succeed within myself
5) I became physically stronger
6) My body became more toned
7) My metabolism received a kickstart every day
8) Tracking the numbers became a satisfying act in itself
9) I felt a boost in my self-confidence

My first set was only ten push-ups, but after a few days, I progressed to twenty. As I became stronger and more toned, I was able to increase my opening set by factors of ten every two to three weeks until I was finally able to achieve the full 100 push-ups in one set. I felt like a great success and still marvel at my own body's ability to do this when I consider my humble beginnings.

ACTION ITEM FOR THIS CHAPTER:

Define the habits you need to build and "Just Start" by pairing them with other habits. Conversely, shed those bad habits by unpairing them from things you love.

Take up the 100-push-up challenge - you will be amazed at your own progress and how good you will feel. It doesn't matter how good the push-ups are, and it doesn't matter what type of push-ups you do.

Take up the 100-push-up challenge - you will be amazed at your own progress and how good you will feel.

Chapter 5

Using your outside voice

Do you know how much time you spend talking to yourself each day?

I wanted to find a credible source to answer this question and was intrigued to discover that the science behind this phenomenon is broad, and the results are varied. Eventually, I found William James, who has been named the "Father of American Psychology." William James is credited with being the first educator to offer a psychology course in the United States. One of his quotes is, "A great many people think they are thinking when they are merely rearranging their prejudices."

It appears that around 99% of our thoughts are utterly useless and generally involve us worrying about things that we have no control over or contemplating things we should be doing but don't do. Only one percent is valuable because it involves problem-solving and understanding the knowledge we attain.

Do you know what else is happening in your life while you're inside your own head? Nothing! Remember that we have sixteen hours available to us in a day to accomplish something of value. How much of that time do you think we typically spend inside our own heads debating about past occurrences, trying to decide what to do right now, and worrying about the future?

Why do we spend time arguing with ourselves?

I'd like to share a routine from one of my favourite comedians, Steven Wright. Steven states in relation to talking to oneself, "I was talking to myself the other day, but I could tell I was lying, so I said, "You're full of sh!t." and I said, "What?" and I said, "Nothing." The point I'm trying to make is that it highlights the absurdity of engaging with ourselves endlessly. We win the argument when we resolve to do something positive for our lives and then take the necessary action. We lose the argument when we decide to do nothing and therefore receive no benefit.

I remember very distinctly arguing with myself on many occasions when I was trying to build up the motivation to go to the gym or for a run. My inside voice told me that I should wait until after dinner to exercise, while my opposing argument was that I should exercise first and then have dinner afterward. I would go back and forth in my own mind arguing this point. I already knew that the right answer was to exercise first because my motivation and ability to exercise after dinner would be significantly diminished; however, the part of me that argued in favour of delaying seemed to win most of the time. This drove me crazy! How could this be?

Why is it that our inside voice wants us to do the least amount of work?

Our self-talk does not seem to have our best interests in mind. It feels like an unmotivated child that just wants us to follow the path of least resistance and survive on the minimal amount of work, or worse still, no work at all. This voice hates change and steers us away from challenges. It is not a voice that is going to support us in achieving success.

So, if we know, we spend the vast majority of our time inside our own heads, and if we know that self-talk is predominantly interested in keeping us subdued and unsuccessful, we must surely recognize the need to take action and more direct control of our lives. We need to take its power away.

Does our outside voice tell us something different than the inside voice?

The moment we start speaking out loud, we attract our own attention and actively listen to ourselves. It's an unusual phenomenon but one that's easy to prove. Just try it right now (but consider the appropriateness of your immediate surroundings). Start by saying your own name and telling yourself something. You will feel your motivation snap to attention.

You see, we *do* respond very well to external stimuli. Self-talk is not very engaging, but an external voice, even if it's our own, does impact our hearing in the same way that it does if someone else is speaking to us. The only thing that's different is that we recognize and trust (hopefully) ourselves.

When we speak out loud to ourselves, there are two things that we recognize immediately:

1) We know if we hear the truth or a lie

2) We know that our motivation must be for our benefit, that we don't have ulterior motives

Why is it important to look at ourselves?

Have you ever just stood and looked at yourself in the mirror? I'm not talking about seeing ourselves when we fix our hair, shave, or apply makeup. I'm talking about looking in the mirror for the express purpose of looking ourselves in the eyes and thinking about what we see and how we feel about it. I can tell you that pre-weight loss, I avoided looking at myself in the mirror. I did not like what I saw and felt shame and guilt. Some of this was because I had let myself get out of control, but some were because I had childhood guilt and shame that I had not let go of and could see if I let myself look directly in the mirror.

If we don't like what we see in the mirror, how can we like anyone else? Looking at ourselves is a way of letting us know if we've dealt with our root causes. When we can look at ourselves in the mirror and smile easily, we know that we have progressed to a good place. It's not only our faces that give us insight, but also our body language that shows us how we're feeling about ourselves. Take the time to do this every day. It only takes a few moments and is a great barometer for how we are truly feeling.

Are the eyes the window to the soul? If so, then we should be looking intently into our own souls...

Why can we trust our outside voice?

If we can accept that we waste most of our time on thoughts that take us nowhere, then we can also understand that we need to get out of our own heads to take action. Our inside voice is the one that wants us to stay safe and never take a risk, never change a habit, never try, and never achieve anything.

Has anyone ever felt truly energized when listening to the old, internal narratives of their inside voice? There is nobody that can truly hear it, not even you. There is nobody to see it, even if we're looking in the mirror.

When you declare something with your outside voice, you feel motivated, empowered, and confident. You create aural and visual cues for yourself to prompt real actions.

If you use a tool like the five-second rule to help you to "Just Start" and then perform the countdown out loud, you will become more motivated to take action. In my past, I would avoid waking up at any cost as I wanted more than anything else to get more sleep. I realized that if I did not speak out loud, it was

If we don't like what we see in the mirror, how can we like anyone else?

much easier to stay in my sleepy state, but the moment I began speaking out loud, my body and brain would respond quickly, making a return to sleep all but impossible. Back then, I was deliberately trying not to take action, and my negative self-talk was the master. Now, I have the tools to succeed and achieve, so I flipped this script and used my outside voice to inspire and energize me to action.

Is it valuable to record our outside voice for later use?

We don't find it unusual to keep recordings of inspirational speeches by famous people, and with the internet, we can look up any motivational speech from anybody at any time, so why not keep recordings of our speeches to ourselves? One thing that is different is that these speeches are made by us, for us, and are specifically designed to help us. A great personal pep talk can hold a significant amount of value.

I often give myself an inspirational speech in front of the mirror in the morning, and I feel energized and motivated to achieve my goals, but sometimes, I surprise myself with a speech that impacts me so much that I regret I didn't record it so I could replay those exact words when I may feel more in need of them. I recorded some inspirational words for a coaching group I'm part of and posted it to a group chat some time ago. I recently came across that post and watched it several weeks after I had shared it. I felt the same enthusiasm and energy that I did when I made the recording, and it occurred to me that I could be doing this as often as I'd like. In fact, this could be considered a great form of journaling and provide me with a way to compare how I felt at some point in the past with how I am doing today.

A great personal pep talk can hold a significant amount of value.

What did my internal voice cost me?

If 99% of our time inside our heads is of no value, then in my case, about 98% of this time was spent on the couch. Without the tools I've learned and am sharing with you, I would still be on my couch, inside my head, overweight, and living day to day in constant mourning for the life I never lived. My internal voice was the king of procrastination, and it had become adept at knowing how to win. The waxing and waning of my motivation to change my life gave me small pockets of valuable time to learn and make the adjustments and develop the skills which I now freely share with you so that you can master keeping it off and never go back.

ACTION ITEM FOR THIS CHAPTER:

Stop wasting time. Get out of your head by using, listening to, and trusting your outside voice to inspire and motivate you.

Look at yourself in the mirror and tell yourself what to do, and then act on this inspiration. When you do this, remember to tell yourself how great you are, creating a positive feedback loop!

Chapter 6

Falling off the wagon

What does it mean to fall off the wagon?

This term came about during the temperance movement of the nineteenth century, when it was believed that alcohol consumption was the cause of many societal problems. During this era, water wagons would travel the streets to keep the dust levels down. The expression was coined in reference to it being preferable to drink from the water wagon than to drink alcohol. The expression "falling off the wagon" signified that one had failed to keep a temperance pledge. In modern times, the term is used more broadly to describe the act of failing to adhere to something we have committed to, whether it be abstinence from alcohol or adherence to a health regime such as a diet.

For the purposes of this book, we refer to the "wagon" as the lifestyle we want to live to stay in alignment with our goals. The "wagon" should be a place that we want to be, and the idea of falling off the "wagon" should not be greeted with positive emotions. The more appealing it feels to "fall off the wagon", the more it is likely to occur.

One thing we can agree on is that the idea of "falling off the wagon" is one we associate with failure, guilt, and shame. Every time we do, we regret it, but maybe only in hindsight which is why it's so important for us to have a strong sense of self-awareness so that we limit the ability for it to sneak up on us. After all, it's OUR "wagon", so we should be in control of it.

Isn't there a less painful way to get off the "wagon"?

It seems that the phrase "falling off the wagon" is consistently used regardless of what the failure is in relation to or what the severity of the failure is. You only need to visualize this phrase or watch some old western movies to get the sense that this is a painful scenario.

After many years of struggling with weight loss, I can attest to the fact that "falling off the wagon" is going to happen. Despite all our best intentions, we are going to "fall off the wagon" at some point, and likely more than once. So, does it have to be such a painful experience, and does it have to lead to a failure in our progress towards our goals? It should not.

Most of the pain experienced in "falling off the wagon" comes because we were not prepared, and the event seemed to happen without warning. If we know it's going to happen at some point, why not be prepared for it? Why not plan our periodic departure from the "wagon" so that it's less of a "falling off" and more of a "stepping down"?

Do we need to live on the "wagon" 24/7?

The "wagon" belongs to us, and it is built on our dreams and goals. It is the vehicle that will drive us into our desired future. We set it up as the perfect path to freedom, which means we don't load it up with things that may hinder our progress; however, we are human, and we need a break sometimes. Sometimes we need a vacation, and the longer we go without one, the more appealing it becomes.

Why not plan our periodic departure from the "wagon" so that it's less of a "falling off" and more of a "stepping down"?

Stepping off the "wagon" from time to time can be a great way to reward ourselves and help strengthen our resolve to continue our journey. Not having a plan for departing the "wagon" is a scary concept for me. I would much rather plan when and how it's going to happen. This enables me to enjoy the experience rather than seeing it as a total disaster that I might regret for days afterward, all the while thinking of myself as a failure.

Looking forward to a "stepping off the wagon", more popularly termed a "cheat day," can give us the strength to persevere and reduce the feelings of missing out. When I plan for this, I am much more responsible and can take pleasure in it more because feelings of guilt and shame haunt me. Also, I am still the one in control, so I don't feel like my freedom has been hijacked.

Where is the "wagon" going? Do we want to be left behind?

There is zero value in feeling stress, worry, or guilt in "falling off the wagon". It's going to happen at some point, and the damage it does to achieving our goals may not be especially significant. The real damage will occur if we don't get right back *on* the "wagon" after our minor indiscretion, whether planned or not.

Falling off the wagon is inevitable, so have a plan for getting back on quickly. Minimize the damage through good planning.

Sometimes a "cheat day" may not result in any harm to our health, depending on how it's handled, but I can guarantee that a "cheat weekend" is going to hurt you physically and may bring about feelings of despair and hopelessness that put you at risk of not getting back *on* the "wagon". We know where this path leads, so let's avoid it at all costs. The more time we spend "off the wagon," the harder it becomes to get back *on* again. The "wagon" feels like it's traveled further away from us.

One thing that we should keep in mind is how often we feel the need to step off the "wagon". If we find we "need" to do it frequently, then we may need to analyze our life because it should not be a difficult choice. We should be enjoying our "wagon ride", and the last thing we want to do is restrict ourselves beyond our ability to enjoy it long-term. Remember that we already did the work to lose weight, and now we want to enjoy our life and live our dreams while ensuring we are still keeping it off.

What is Steak Day, and why does it work?

I discovered the concept of Steak Day during one of my many diets. I am deliberately refraining from talking about the different diets. I've tried many and feel that they all have merit, and if you have lost weight, then you have all found the one that worked best for you. Steak Day is a concept or a tool that anyone can employ at any stage of a weight maintenance program. So long as steak is a food that is acceptable to your life choices, it can be a lifesaver to get back on the "wagon" after an accidental or planned departure.

The time to do a Steak Day is the day after you've "fallen off the wagon". More specifically, I recommend a Steak Day if you wake up the following morning and have gained two or more pounds due to an indiscretion the day before. When I say indiscretion, I generally talk about bad culinary choices - food, beverage, or both. If employed successfully, the weight you gained yesterday will be gone tomorrow. It's that simple, but it's not always easy. It must be done the very next day, which is why planning for a "cheat day" is so important. If I am planning to step off the wagon on a Friday night, the first thing I ask myself is: "Am I able to do a Steak Day on Saturday?" If the answer is no, then I choose a different day to step off the "wagon".

This is the process to follow to successfully complete a Steak Day for the temporary weight gain to disappear the following day: Do not eat all day. You can drink as much water, tea, and coffee as you see fit. (Lots of water is encouraged). For dinner, eat the biggest steak that you can manage. The steak does not need to be lean as fat does not have a nullifying impact on this protocol, and cooking it with oil is also acceptable. With the steak, you will eat one whole raw tomato or one whole apple. (It's your preference which you choose. I always chose the tomato myself as it just seemed more appropriate as a pairing for a steak dinner.) This is the only meal permitted for the day.

Eating the steak at the end of the day lets your body know that the supply of food has not been cut off and gives your body permission to let go of whatever is being held from the previous day. The tomato or apple acts as a diuretic, helping your body to eliminate built-up fluids and releasing them through your urine.

I've not been very successful in finding solid scientific data to support why this works, but I have plenty of personal experience and empirical data to confirm that it does work consistently. I would not recommend; however, a lifestyle that requires you do a Steak Day more than once a week. This could be a sign that your "wagon" lifestyle is too restrictive for you.

Why is it easier to say "wait" than to say "no"?

After endless hours, days, weeks, and years of observing my bad behaviour, I could recognize that I was a master at procrastinating from doing things that were good for me, such as exercise, eating responsibly, pursuing my goals, etc. I decided that I needed to employ this same expertise to my benefit rather than my detriment. I turned the art of procrastination into a positive, powerful tool to get back my control and have more freedom and success in my life.

I turned the art of procrastination into a positive, powerful tool to get back my control and have more freedom and success in my life.

After working our way through the first five chapters, we should now understand the mental and physical challenges we need to overcome. However, we can expect cravings to creep up on us from time to time. When this occurs, it can be very difficult to tell ourselves "No". What if we tell ourselves to wait instead, it doesn't seem so bad. While "No" is an outright rejection, "Wait" is just a delay that is much more palatable as it leaves us with the belief that we can still have what we want eventually. The idea is to get us through the craving to the point when we don't mind rejecting whatever the temptation was. As we discussed previously, our motivation can have erratic peaks and valleys, and when we are in a valley, it's hard to say "No"; instead we can delay. Once the craving has passed and our motivation is high again, we can more easily say, "No."

Stall when you're weak and reject when you're strong. This will eventually become a habit to the extent that you will barely even notice it happening. However, if you do fail in this, there is always Steak Day.

A similar concept is recognizing the difference between something you're not allowed to do and something you don't like to do. This can also be expressed in direct relation to food in the following way: For many years, I told myself that I liked pizza, but I couldn't have it because it was bad for my health. What I was inadvertently doing was creating a craving for pizza that I couldn't indulge in. (Cravings that you're never allowed to indulge in do not create happiness...) Later, I resolved the stress of this situation by redefining the word "like" in relation to this scenario. I decided to define something I "liked" as something that was good for me, or something that is good for "most" of me. Pizza was good for my taste buds, but it was not good for my health or my weight, or my digestive system. There are many other foods that made my body feel good *and* taste great. These are the foods that I "liked." I no

Stall when you're weak and reject when you're strong. This will eventually become a habit to the extent that you will barely even notice it happening.

longer needed to tell myself that I couldn't have pizza. I just told myself that I didn't like it based on my new definition. Today, I do not feel that I am missing out on anything because those things that I previously decided I couldn't have are no longer things that I like.

Can "Just Start" work in any situation?

Even though we are well past the beginning of your journey now, it's important to remember that the concept of "Just Start" can and should be used throughout your life.

In fact, the tools in the first chapter can be vital in helping you get back "on the wagon" quickly so that you can continue your journey with little or no damage or delay in your ride to success.

How many ways did I find to "fall off the wagon"? Should I have become a stunt man?

I have "fallen off the wagon" so many times that I could be a stuntman. I am sure I have explored every possible way I can think of to "fall off the wagon", and I literally have the scars to prove it.

I want you to think of yourself as the movie star, and I am your stuntman. I have taken the falls and the pain on your behalf so that you don't have to. Every time you avoid the pain of "falling off the wagon", it makes the failures and pain I went through worth every bump, bruise, and broken bone!

ACTION ITEM FOR THIS CHAPTER:

Remember to stall when you're weak and reject when you're strong.

Redefine the things you like based on things that are good for you, not just things that taste good or feel good.

Chapter 7

Embrace the competitor within

What is competition, and how can it be valuable?

Most people are aware of this famous quote, "Never criticize a man until you've walked a mile in his shoes." Jokingly, there was a second part that I added to this quote, using it as a mantra for many years now: "Never criticize a man until you've walked a mile in his shoes, that way when you do criticize him, you're a mile away and you have his shoes." To me, this speaks to the essence of competition. Our success can be greatly enhanced by taking every advantage we can find.

Anyone who reads this book is in a place to relate to each other very well. Nobody else can really understand what we've been through. We had fought very hard to recover our lives back to the place we were in before things started to slide. In most cases, it took a monumental effort. I am sure we can agree that we want to create every single opportunity for success that is available to us over the long-term, and create the success that we have determined belongs to us.

You may think you're not a competitive person, but is that true?

Whether we believe ourselves to be competitive or not, we cannot deny that we have been in heavy competition with ourselves ever since we embarked on our weight loss journey. It is likely that our own bad habits and inside voice have been in fierce competitors with our true selves that wanted to achieve something good in our lives. At some point, we've all been in competition for a job, a sport, or even for a spouse. With only a quick look at the world of online dating, it is easy to see how a "swipe left" or "swipe right" culture pits us all against each other in the quest to be "chosen" by a potential mate.

Have you ever played a board game like Scrabble, Monopoly, or Settlers of Catan? If so, you likely have a competitive nature. We may agree to play these games with the thought that we are doing it to have fun and fellowship with friends and family, and this is a fair and reasonable thought to have; however, none of us start playing any game with the thought that we are trying to lose. In fact, every one of these games are structured around the concept of winning. To win, we must beat somebody which means someone else will lose. While this may go against the concept of equity, someone is always going to lose, and someone is always going to win. It should be you that wins!

Is everything a competition?

Every time we make a decision, we are weighing various options and then choosing one of those options. Sometimes we choose a good option, and sometimes we choose a bad option: Do I go to the gym, or do I stay home and pour a glass of wine? Quite often our choices are between what we want to do right now and what we know is best for us. Many times, whatever seems most fun and delivers an enjoyable outcome most quickly, is the one that we choose, to our detriment.

If we can have the self-awareness to recognize that critical moment that we are faced with, we can use that moment to create a competition and engage that natural competitive spirit to drive us to make choices that move us towards our goals.

Sometimes this competition comes down to a simple question: "What do I want *now* versus what do I want *most*?"

This question is sometimes referred to when considering the definition of discipline. When we have "competing" wants and desires, we naturally have competition.

Whose responsibility is it to achieve our goals?

It's of vital importance to recognize that our dreams and goals belong to us and nobody else. Our dreams are ours alone to achieve and nobody is coming to save us. If all else falls apart, the accountability for our success or failure lies with ourselves alone.

We can get the support of family, friends, coaches, courses, support groups, etc., but we must be careful not to rely too heavily on any of these. At some point, we are going to be on our own in this journey, if only in our minds, and we are the only ones that can ensure we are never going away any time soon. It is always us that we see in the mirror, so we need to embrace the fact that we are our number one accountability partner.

How can we align with others to improve our chances of success?

Every single person that picks up this book has something in common with each other: we have all gained then lost weight and are now determined to never go back. Finding others with common goals is a great way of recognizing that we are not alone and that our struggles are not unique. This alone is not only comforting, but also gives us the confidence to strive for success.

Somebody, somewhere, is going to be in the same place as you. Maybe they are a little further behind, and maybe they are a little further ahead. You can connect with others to find your long-term success. You can also align with others and help support each other through ideas, strategies, and tools that will help you and others. I am sharing the key tools that have helped me in my journey, and many of them will be foundational for your success as well as others, but there will be other tools that also work well for you that you can learn and employ in your journey.

It is rare to find that you are going through something unique. One key to your recovery is to seek out and find those that have paved the way and learn from their experience to help you in your journey. You have already sought out and found this book; whether by design or by chance, you can take the insights that work best for you and employ them for your own success. While you are the ultimate authority on your own journey, joining a community is comforting and can serve as a cushion when your motivation is low, and your frustration is high. We are all meant to be in relationship with each other, and we should never forego this privilege and basic human need.

How did I create competition to succeed?

One thing I found was that I needed to constantly find new ways to compete with others to help me stay motivated to succeed. You see, I couldn't control the drive or the goals of those I would compete against. Sometimes they just stopped what they were doing, and sometimes they achieved their final goals, so they basically "exited" the game we were playing, whether they knew they were in competition with me or not.

Sometimes when we compete, we can become discouraged if we are not performing as well as we would like. What if the person we chose to compete against was doing better than we were? Do we feel a desire to give up? We need to remember that our success is measured by our own achievement and not that of the other person. This concept is best told with this story of an old friend of mine that I will share as a cautionary tale.

As a teenager, I was involved in competitive swimming. I was not very successful, but I always aspired to be better. My friend Lisa was a natural swimmer, and she was fast. I was jealous, but thankfully I was never in direct competition with her. Lisa was in direct competition with another girl; however, and this girl consistently beat Lisa in every competition. As strong and talented as Lisa was, she always finished second to this other girl. Over time Lisa became discouraged and quit the competition because she felt she wasn't good enough. Well, you could imagine how one might feel years later to see this "other girl" become an Olympic gold medallist in multiple events? I know that I would not feel so bad in coming second to such a successful competitor. At the time, however, Lisa could not have known this which is why it's important to measure our success against ourselves and not against others. Using someone else to help motivate ourselves is great, but my success is for me and not measured by others' achievements. Someone else is always faster, stronger, leaner, richer, etc., but I can still be great regardless.

For a personal example of my own, I have a friend named Adrian whom I met as part of an executive coaching program. I am a little taller and of a broader build than Adrian. We were both striving for some weight loss, amongst other goals. I knew that I should be able to lose weight faster than him. While he never appeared to be competing against me (I later found out that he was), I was clear with him that I was competing against him. I would check in with him regularly to see where he was at, and I "used" him to help drive my motivation and success. Throughout our journeys, we had several discussions on strategies that were working and those that were not. The relationship and success we both enjoyed were satisfying and added an extra dimension of accountability to my daily routines and habits. I keep in touch with him to this day to see how he is

Remember to measure your success against your own goals and not those of others.

doing, partly because I want him to be successful and partly because I want to keep myself motivated.

ACTION ITEMS FOR THIS CHAPTER:

Find a way to create a competition that inspires you to succeed, and then begin competing.

Remember to measure your success against your own goals and not those of others.

Chapter 8

The scale is your friend

How do you know you've lost weight, and how do you know if you're keeping it off?

Since we've all been through a weight loss journey, one time or many times, we have all used a scale to measure our success. If we didn't use a scale, then how did we know we had lost the weight? While it's true we could have used some more indirect methods, weighing ourselves is the most reliable and accurate measuring tool we have for this purpose.

While our main goal is no longer to lose weight, we still need to use measurement tools to help keep us on track and prevent any backward sliding and take corrective action early. To give up using the scale once we've achieved our weight loss goal is a mistake that I have made many times to my sincere regret and frustration.

In a Cornell University 2015 study, Dr. David Levitsky found that among people who were trying to lose weight, those who weighed themselves daily and recorded their results lost about three percent of their body weight on average over the course of a year. In comparison, people who did not weigh themselves daily did not see a significant change in their weight on average.

Moreover, after that year, the people who weighed themselves daily were able to maintain their weight loss for another year which is important because maintaining a new, lower weight without gaining pounds back tends to be more difficult for people than losing weight, according to the research.

"There are thousands of ways of losing weight," said Dr. David Levitsky, a professor of nutrition and psychology at Cornell University. "Losing weight is not the problem, but to maintain that weight loss is the problem."

We always want to choose the "right tool for the right job", right?

The "right tool for the right job" is an old adage that is very appropriate for us in this situation.

If you're a Canadian, you may be familiar with a TV show called the Red Green Show. The common theme of this show is that you can use duct tape to fix or build anything. While this may be true in general, the results are often substandard and can be far from ideal.

Our problem was weight gain, and it was most easily measured with a scale. Keeping it off requires the same tool. It really is that simple.

What can the scale tell us other than just our weight?

In very basic terms, our scale tells us if we have lost weight, gained weight, or stayed the same weight. The moment we have this measure, we can decide what this information means. If we lost, gained, or maintained from the previous day's measurement, we have a small window of time where we can analyze what we've done in the past twenty-four hours, determine what contributed to what we see on the scale today, and take corrective action if need be. This information is extremely valuable to us, and we shouldn't pass up the opportunity to take advantage of an easy data analysis that can help inform our future choices.

Losing weight is not the problem, but to maintain that weight loss is the problem.

We could break this analysis into two easy categories: singular events and trend analysis extending over time. An example of a singular event could be that you ate a certain food yesterday and it impacted you in either a positive or negative way the next morning on the scale. An example of a trend analysis could be that you notice when you go to sleep at a reasonable time each night, you tend to lose some weight through attaining proper rest for your body.

One thing I noticed over time is that I have a "superpower" that enables me to gain incredible amounts of weight overnight if I ate noodles or ice cream the day before. Thankfully I have Steak Day to combat this when it occurs. While this data could be gleaned from a singular event, sometimes we have multiple singular events occur in a day, so monitoring over time is required to whittle this down to find the root cause. Once discovered, I can put plans in place to deal with it. It doesn't mean I can never eat noodles or ice cream, just that I can be more deliberate about planning for it by organizing a Steak Day for the following day or by being conscious of the time of day I consume certain foods. It does make a difference.

Is it safe to measure your success by how your clothes fit?

I've spoken to many people about the concept of using the look and fit of their clothes as their measuring tool for weight loss or weight maintenance. My only conclusion is that this method scares me beyond belief, and I don't think it's effective at all.

Some recent examples of this come to mind as people all over the world deal with a work-from-home culture. Many office-based workers have begun to do their work from home; thus the requirements for usual office attire were thrown out the window. At best, this only requires them to be "presentable" for

How our clothes fit is truly a lagging indicator that we should not rely on if we want to remain successful after our weight loss.

the laptop camera which usually only requires the top half of your torso to be visible. (A special note of advice here if it's not already too late - be very conscious of not standing up during a video meeting without considering what attention you've given to your bottom half!) Anyways, many found that after several months of this work-from-home environment when they tried on their "bottom half" work attire, their clothes did not fit nearly as well as they used to. This generally prompted a search for the scale and the subsequent revelation that they had gained anywhere between ten and twenty pounds. Thankfully, we can prevent this.

I am sure I already know the answer to this question, but I will ask you anyway: Would you rather find out that you've just gained two pounds or twenty pounds? It's almost a rhetorical question, I know. In general, because this can vary with gender, height, age, and build, we can easily gain ten pounds with no impact on the fit of our clothes. Do we really want to find out one day that we've regained ten pounds and need to do the work again to get back to where we want to be? How our clothes fit is truly a lagging indicator that we should not rely on if we want to remain successful after our weight loss.

If we used a scale to record our weight loss, a loss which was much harder to achieve, then why wouldn't we use a scale to help protect against gaining weight back, a gain which is much easier to achieve? This should not even be a question we need to consider; the answer is obvious.

Is it easier for us to gain the weight back than it is for others to gain weight for the first time?

The unfortunate thing about fat cells is that they do not diminish in number as we lose weight. They are always there and can be "refilled" at a moment's notice. Outside of liposuction, we are not able to remove the number of fat cells in our body. Through our weight gain, we have stretched and filled our fat cells. In the case of extreme weight gain, it is even suggested that we may have generated additional fat cells during this time which also do not disappear after weight loss.

We must remain ever vigilant as our bodies have been there once (or twice or more), and we definitely do not want to go back - ever. While it can be seen as a bothersome and tiring burden, we can take the positive spin that we are simply looking after our health just as anyone else might do. Because we know where a lack of vigilance can lead, we can recognize the importance of this tracking.

Are we in danger of letting the scale become an obsession?

OK, fair enough. I know we are not in a group setting together, but indulge me here. Put your hand up if you've ever gotten into the habit of weighing yourself multiple times per day and felt the highs and lows as the scale weight moved up and down, sometimes fluctuating wildly. Don't be embarrassed as this is a common phenomenon. While we are losing weight, the scale becomes this all-powerful entity that determines, day by day, if we are on track for success, so we give it the power to influence how we feel.

Setting our goals and tracking our success is important, but we likely never set milestones that include hourly or daily measurements. Perhaps we have a goal of not going over a certain weight, and Steak Day can help us manage any glitches we experience, but we want to ensure our goals are realistic and achievable without creating daily stress in our lives. We always want to make sure we are living first.

We want to ensure our goals are realistic and achievable without creating daily stress in our lives. We always want to make sure we are living first.

What new ways can we find to measure our success to complement our scale?

As I was on my weight loss journey, all double digits of them, one thing I found extremely valuable was having a scale that measured body fat. I know that both men and women experience body fat fluctuations in unique and impactful ways. The metabolisms of men and women can sometimes differ significantly. Many women I have talked to about this have expressed their shock and horror at the lack of downward progress in their weight as their bodies tended to retain water or experience hormone fluctuations at different stages of their lives. Most men I spoke with were experiencing their water retention in relation to heavy weightlifting activities in the gym. Either way, we will all experience weight fluctuations at different times and for different reasons. This leads us to seek out supplemental ways of measuring our success.

There are several ways we can measure our body fat. Let's look at the top methods and how they work so, we can each determine individually the one that is most convenient for us. I cannot tell you what a comfort it is to me to know that a lack of weight gain, or worse still, a weight increase, may only be water retention and temporary in nature. It is good to know that I don't have to take any serious actions to correct a problem that doesn't really exist. I've excluded methods that require professional services as you want to be able to take measurements on a regular basis. Ideally, every day in the morning before you eat or drink anything and after you have purged your system is best (this is the least personal way I could think of to state this).

1) **Skin Calipers:** a simple device is used to "pinch" folds of skin at various locations on your body. You record the thickness of the skin at each of these locations, make a simple calculation, and your body fat percentage is determined from this. The

calipers are not expensive to buy, and with some effort, you can pinch and measure the skin areas without assistance (although it's helpful to have someone pinch the skin fold on your back).

2) **Bioelectric Impedance Analysis (BIA)** is the simplest and least intrusive. Many bathroom scales come with this feature nowadays, along with other body measurement features like bone density, muscle density, and body water percentage. The scale sends a small, non-intrusive electrical pulse through the body and the speed of the impulse determines the body fat percentage. Since lean muscle tissue conducts electricity faster than fat, it is a simple way to measure the level of body fat in the body.

3) **Body Mass Index (BMI)** is probably the most well-known method to measure body fat, and the most unreliable and misleading, in my humble opinion. The problem with BMI is it does not take into account the build of the person being measured. Our builds are so varied that using BMI is just not going to help you at all. Remember, BMI is used as a measurement of excess body weight, not excess body fat. Relying on the results produced by the BMI method is going to make some people happy and some people sad, and they may each be completely misled because of the limitations of this system.

While I use both calipers and BIA, I have found that BIA is the simplest method by far; it can be used every day and can give you a consistent reading each morning. While it's true that each method could give a slightly misleading number, once you are using one method consistently, that method will be completely accurate from the perspective that you can see the CHANGE in the reading from day to day. It is a change that commands our attention to take action as needed.

ACTION ITEMS FOR THIS CHAPTER:

Your scale is a great tool. Purchase a good one and use the information it provides to your benefit.

Beware that some scales advertise that they measure BIA, but do not. The extra time to research and find a good scale is worth the effort. You will likely get what you pay for.

If we blame someone else for something that is impacting us negatively, we will not take responsibility for dealing with that issue.

Chapter 9

Take responsibility for everything

What happens when we blame someone else for something that impacts us?

I want to begin this chapter by sharing a quote from one of my favourite authors, as I think it sets the scene perfectly. Clinical psychologist Dr. Henry Cloud wrote an anecdote in his book 'Necessary Endings' about a married couple that came to see him get some help for their adult son who had "so many problems." He couldn't hold down a job. He indulged in drugs. He was lazy. He was living at home. He had so many problems that they frustratingly conveyed to Dr. Cloud in detail. After hearing their concerns, Dr. Cloud stated, "It sounds like he doesn't have any problems at all. It sounds like you need to let him have some problems."

There is one thing we can all confidently agree on here. If we blame someone else for something that is impacting us negatively, we will not take responsibility for dealing with that issue. After all, it's somebody else's responsibility. We are really saying to ourselves, "I am not happy with something, but I am not prepared to deal with it myself."

The moment we blame someone else for anything that impacts us negatively, we are effectively resigning ourselves to leaving any possible solutions in the hands of someone that may not have what's best for us in their minds or hearts. Generally, people will do what is best for themselves first and then consider what is best for others.

There is a famous quote by Abraham Lincoln that I will shorten to this - "I don't like man. I must get to know him better." There are two simple concepts in this quote. Firstly, President Lincoln is being negatively impacted by someone else. In this case, he does not like someone. He may not feel much discomfort in this, but he does acknowledge that he does not have positive feelings towards a person. The subject of his dislike, the man he doesn't like, may be entirely oblivious to the situation, leaving President Lincoln as the only person holding negative feelings in this situation. Secondly, President Lincoln, in a very direct way, resolves immediately to be the one to take responsibility. He did not lay blame on the other person, even though he held negative feelings towards that person. If you might be unwilling to take my advice, at least take that of President Lincoln.

Who was responsible when you lost weight?

Taking responsibility can be difficult. The bigger the problem, the harder it can be to step up and take responsibility for it. When problems arise, they sometimes happen suddenly. Correcting or dealing with a problem can take courage, commitment, work, planning, and discipline.

One thing we should all be able to acknowledge is that we took responsibility for losing weight. Somehow, we were the ones that stepped up and took charge. The result was a successful weight loss, and this happened because we decided and achieved something important to us.

I really love the benefit of hindsight. Looking back at things that have transpired, and taking the time to think about them, has given me many great revelations about myself and about how I can better achieve my goals going forward.

Here is one important thing I have found to be true in almost every aspect of my life. The first person to take responsibility for a

The first person to take responsibility for a problem is also the person who can take charge of dealing with the problem.

problem is also the person who can take charge of dealing with the problem.

At first, this may not seem like it would be a positive thing. It may seem like a lot of work. Keep in mind, though, that the person that steps up to fix something gets to be the one who decides when to fix something, how to fix something, what is involved, what the result should look like, and to make sure it actually happens.

When I take responsibility for something, I experience a great sense of relief and empowerment. I feel like I am taking control of my life.

What are the outside forces that are influencing your success, and how can you deal with them?

It feels great when we have everything in our lives going well, such as finances, fitness, family, and faith (4 important "F's"). When we are riding our "wagon" with confidence and everything is going our way, we may sometimes be hit upon something unexpected that threatens to upset our routines, and we are forced to react. In fact, this is not something that may sometimes occur, but something we should expect because it's going to happen.

Someone may say something as simple as, "You're too skinny!" Have you ever had someone tell you this? While on face value, it seems like a great compliment, it also can derail us. When someone close to us tells us that we've lost too much weight, we may feel compelled to listen to them, ceasing some good health habits and/or adding some bad habits just because we want to acknowledge their opinion.

Keep in mind that we may "fall off the wagon", but we should be committed to getting back on quickly.

In the case where this happened to me, it came from people in my life who were, and always had been, slimmer than myself. As I lost weight and slowly became skinnier than them, I believe they realized that they were now overweight in comparison to me and unconsciously wanted me to stop losing weight out of fear that they would feel compelled to address their own weight issues. Suddenly, I was the one in shape, and this created a subconscious threat to the normal order of things.

We can so easily be influenced by others, but if we are truly taking full responsibility, we can be mindful that others may attempt to influence us negatively, whether they are conscious of this or not. Sometimes it might be something more direct and more harmful, like the loss of a job or a health problem. Whatever it is going to be, we can be sure that it is going to threaten to derail the progress we have made, upset our habits, and challenge our discipline.

Keep in mind that we may "fall off the wagon", but we should be committed to getting back on quickly. We can mitigate the chance of bad things happening to us by being conscious of our choices, but we will be showing strength and courage when we maintain our discipline through any adversity that may arise.

Can I take responsibility for things that just happen to me? If I do this, does it make me free?

I always used to think of freedom as the absence of responsibility. The fewer responsibilities I had, the more freedom I believed I had. In hindsight, I was wrong. Oxford dictionary defines freedom as: "the power or right to act, speak, or think as one wants without hindrance or restraint." When I reviewed this definition, I realized that I had been focusing on the second half of the definition, and now understand that the true base of freedom comes from the first part of the definition.

The Jason L Schembri of today takes responsibility for everything he can. This is me exercising my "power" and my "right to act." The moment I take responsibility is the instant I experience my fullest sense of freedom.

When I take control of a situation, I have the freedom to decide what happens next.

If someone else takes responsibility, then I am now relegated to the position of waiting to see what someone else decides as to what will happen next. I don't feel any sense of freedom in this.

What happens when I refuse to be a victim?

There are two elements to this word that are important to understand, and they relate to the past and the present tense. If something bad happened to me in the past, I "was" a victim at that moment in time. If I choose to continue to live in that moment, I am choosing to "be" a victim now. We may not be able to change whether we are the victim of something bad that happened to us, but we are completely free to move past that moment and refuse to carry that victimhood into the present (and future).

One thing I can be sure of is that the time spent "being" a victim is never concurrent with the time spent taking action, improving my situation, taking control, or creating freedom. I didn't lose any weight while I was being a victim. My journey to success began the moment I stopped being a victim.

Winston Churchill has some words of wisdom to help motivate us to not live in victimhood, and they are simple, but powerful: "Never, never, never give up." I believe that every time we give up, we are choosing to be a victim. Nothing good ever happens when we're in this place.

When I take control of a situation, I have the freedom to decide what happens next.

How can I be mindful of when I lose control?

Unfortunately, we are often unaware that we have lost control until after the event. We may not be aware we have "fallen off the wagon" until the moment we hit the ground painfully. On those occasions, the most positive, impactful thing we can do is to get back ON quickly, use the tools we have to recover, and think about what just happened so we can prevent a future occurrence. If we fully recover from a mishap, then perhaps we don't need to do anything except get back on the wagon and carry on. There is no point in dwelling on something that already happened, other than learning from it.

It is not an easy thing to suddenly become mindful. A better practice is to be constantly mindful. While this sounds like work, there are some amazing benefits to this. Firstly, when we are being mindful, the time does not slip away from us we are "noticing" everything going on around us and everything going on within us. We don't miss all the little moments and not only take advantage of them, but also and live them to the maximum benefit.

The practice of any art is what gives us the ability to perform it under pressure. The practice of being aware is what will give us the ability to be mindful in that critical moment when we need to be. We practice a sport regularly so that we can perform in the game.

As Bruce Lee stated, "I fear not the man who has practiced 10,000 kicks once, but I fear the man who has practiced one kick 10,000 times." When the moment arrives that you need to defend yourself, that one kick will be performed intuitively, quickly, and extremely successfully. The same is true for the choices we must make when a critical moment arrives.

How did my life change when I started taking responsibility for everything?

For most of my life, I spent time running away from responsibility. Responsibility made me feel weighed down, suffocated, trapped, and I felt like I was losing all my freedom. Well, the reason I felt this way was because I was taking responsibility for as little as I could. Today, I consciously look for things to take responsibility for. I actively pursue this and feel empowered and free. It gives me the confidence to know that I am the one who will take action to make things better and achieve success.

A spin-off benefit to this, I have noticed, is that by taking responsibility for the things that I truly should, I am making other people's lives better. I am relieving others of the burden and fallout of my problems. I get to be a leader for others and support them. I have become trusted and reliable. I am seen as a man of integrity. Other people like it when I take responsibility and that feedback makes me more excited and committed to keep doing it. There is really no downside here.

ACTION ITEMS FOR THIS CHAPTER:

Taking responsibility for everything you can gives you control, authority, and freedom.

Write a paragraph on what you're already taking responsibility for. Write one more paragraph on something "new" that you should take responsibility for. Now go and take it.

When you take responsibility, it means that someone else does not have to do it for you. This is the perfect building block for great relationships and a great stress release between people. Stress, after all, can lead us to lose control and destroy the life we are building.

Chapter 10

Never go back!

How do I bring these tools together to suit me best?

I live in a small one-bedroom apartment. Honestly, it is smaller than five hundred square feet. When I first walked in, I thought, "this is cozy." It suits me and serves my purposes. I have a small storage room with a toolbox in it. I've accumulated these tools over many years and in many situations. Many of these tools no longer serve any valuable purpose for me, but I keep them anyway, just in case. I only buy a new tool when I have a specific need for it. I wouldn't push tools onto anyone that I wouldn't use myself. I am my own best customer. I've organized the tools in this book into what I believe to be the best combination that one can apply to create maximum success. Take the tools that will work best for you and your situation.

Go to **www.jasonlschembri.com** to find more practical tools that you can use every day to get you started and help keep you successful.

How can I keep on track with this every single day?

Empirical evidence has proven that writing down goals is directly aligned with the achieving those goals. The only conflict in this data is the degree to which writing your goals influences your achievement of them. In every study I read, the number, ratio, or percentage is extremely high. So, write your goals down and write them regularly. Start your day by picking up a journal and "Just Start" writing. Don't worry if you can't think of what to write, even if that means your first words are, "I don't know what to write but...".

Trust me, the more you do this, the more you will find that thoughts and feelings just start flowing out of you, then the next thing you know, you will be exposing important revelations about your life, what you think, what you feel, and how situations and events have impacted you. You will be truly amazed by the things you will learn about yourself by doing this.

How does having a daily plan create freedom?

When you know what you want or need to do in a day and plan for it, you will notice a feeling of strength and freedom. When you recognize and create direction for the day, you will experience a feeling of power and purpose that will give you control of your life.

When you decide on the plan for today, it means that someone else is NOT the one making the plan for YOUR day. When it's you that takes charge, it's you that creates freedom - you get to decide what happens.

How can I make these plans to drive my success?

The first thing we need to establish is what success looks like to us. What is it that I want to achieve that is going to make me truly happy and enable me to live my dreams? From here, I can start setting long-term, medium-term, and short-term goals and create my plan to meet these objectives.

I write and re-write these goals on a regular basis. I keep some of them on a whiteboard, and some are just in a journal or e-notes on my phone. I am reinforcing them constantly in my mind. One exercise I always perform is to review my goals and confirm that they integrate well with each other.

While I write my goals from the top-down, they need to work from the bottom-up too. Does the achievement of the short-term goals help achieve the medium-term goals and so forth? To illustrate how this works for me, I pick one goal and I write it "top-down" then make sure it works from the "bottom-up." Becoming an author was at the top of my list. My daily goals included setting aside time for daily book writing, so each day under the heading of "Dreams," I wrote down at least one action item that would take me closer to becoming an author. On a weekly basis, I tracked, and continue to do so, 90-day goals where I set deadlines to be at a certain place in my writing to make sure I am on track. Without deadlines in place, I will always be at risk of running on a timer that never runs out. This is one of my ways of creating some self-accountability. So, my daily, 90-day, and long-term goals all work together to keep my driving me to achieve my dreams.

How do I know when I'm living my best life?

Pursuing our dreams and achieving our goals are the best pursuits we can engage in, but we can't forget to enjoy the journey. The goal that is achieved in one year cannot be at the expense of one year of unhappiness. (Well, yes, it can, but does that sound like a good use of our time?)

I know when I am living my best life when I combine two key components, and they can both be determined on a daily basis: Firstly, did I have a great day? It's that simple. If I can look back on my day and feel good, then I am living my best life. Secondly, did I move ahead in the pursuit of my dreams and goals? Again, it's simple. If I moved the needle towards achieving something that is important to me, then I lived my best life that day. At any moment, we can step back from ourselves and look at who we are, what we're doing, and where we're going. If everything lines up, then we are living our best lives.

How do I choose the tools that work the best for me?

Have you ever been to a conference? How many keynote addresses, presentations, and workshops did you attend in back-to-back days? How many people did you meet and network with? At the end of all of that, what did you remember, and what knowledge did you retain to the extent that you were able to benefit your life or your career?

Statistically, we only retain about 10% of what we absorb in these situations, and that percentage drops even further when we move into the application into our lives and work, so we want to be deliberate about the knowledge and information that we choose to retain and apply to our lives. Thankfully, we can always refer back to this book to refresh ourselves on a regular basis, but we will still only ever take that which appeals to us and makes sense as a useful tool.

In developing these tools over time, I instinctively knew which tools were going to work best for me. Some of these tools are born of the ideas of others, and it is rare these days to come up with completely original concepts that serve us. In many cases, we adapt tools developed by others to suit our own purposes. I would encourage you to pick and choose what you know immediately will work for you and adapt the rest to best suit your own needs. Throughout this book, I have given acknowledgements to other authors who have inspired me with their ideas and tools and adapted them to suit my needs. I encourage you to do the same for yourself.

What is your daily routine that has brought you success?

When you lost weight, it's very likely that you set yourself a daily routine that worked for you. Perhaps you've gone through a weight loss journey many times and have settled into a routine that has proven successful. I know that my weight loss routine works very well for me and does every time need to employ it. My weight loss routine, however, is much easier to follow than the routine I follow for overall success - after all, the weight loss routine is narrow in focus and short in duration.

I took all my trial-and-error lessons, studied them in detail, got to truly know myself, and brought them together to create the tools I needed to succeed, then tested them and confirmed they worked. My decades-long journey included a lot of frustration, suffering, and disappointment, and I hope to save you as much of this pain as possible. This is really very simple, but again that does not mean it's easy.

The tools in this book were designed to be followed every day and drive you forward, so you can live in the best way possible, a strong place, the place that you were when you won your war and got to where you wanted to be. You have gone through a great battle. We both have, and now it's time to enjoy the spoils of that battle without finding ourselves back in the same battle again.

Here is what I do every day, without fail. It works for me and can work for you. My only goal is for you to succeed. I look forward to hearing about your success, and I am also here to support you in your journey to continued success.

FINAL ACTION ITEMS:

This is my daily routine, and it is intentionally based on each chapter of this book. I follow these steps and write them in a journal every day. They are both reflections and plans. Some can be written at night, and some work better in the morning. There should be something written on each line every day.

1) **The Scale is your friend (chapter 8) – what is my weight today? Did it change from yesterday? If so, why? What did I do that influenced this? What can I learn from this? What can I do today to make a positive impact on the scale for tomorrow?**
2) **Just Start (Chapter 1) – What is something that I know I need to "Just Start" today? This can be something I need to tell myself each day until I make the commitment to do it. This should not be a difficult thing to recognize. It lurks in our minds and is always there. Notice it, think about it, and take action today!**
3) **Eliminating the Root Causes (chapter 2) – this is one of the deepest and most meaningful things we can do every day. Why do we do the things we do? How do these things link to something that happened to us in the past? What is one thing we can do today to deal with one of these root causes? It's likely that there are many of these.**
4) **What are your dreams (chapter 3) – What do I really want in life? What can I do today to move toward my dream?**
5) **Build your habits (chapter 4) – What habit am I currently building? How can I keep building it today? What new habits do I need to build? What bad habit do I need to drop?**
6) **Affirmations (chapter 5) – Stand in front of your mirror and look at yourself. Tell yourself all the things you can think of that are great about you. Tell yourself what you are going to do today and how that will make today an amazing day. You are worthy.**

7) Wagon (chapter 6) – Am I comfortable on my wagon? Am I in danger of falling off? Are there bumps in the road coming up that I need to plan for? Am I ready to get back on the wagon if I fall off today or tomorrow?
8) Competition (chapter 7) – Am I currently in competition with someone? How is that going? What can I do today to compete and win? Do I really want to win? Why or why not?
9) Take responsibility (Chapter 8) – Am I being responsible for the things I should be? Is there one thing today I can focus on taking responsibility for that will make my life and someone else's life better?
10) Daily push-up challenge (chapter 4) – How many push-ups did I do in my first set today? Is it equal to or more than yesterday? Am I working towards 100 in the first set? What can I do to get better at this?

What's next?

Thank you for taking this journey with me through the book that describes ten years of my frustrations, struggles, learnings, and revelations.

I genuinely hope that the stories I've shared, along with the tools and strategies, can help you with your journey and bring some benefit to you.

While our struggles are individual, they don't need to be addressed in solitude. We all need help along the way if we are to find freedom through sustainable weight management.

I have dedicated my life to helping people who struggle with this issue, and I encourage you to connect with me so that we can move forward together as part of a community that supports and challenges each other.

Please get in touch with me through my website www.jasonlschembri.com and on social media under the title JasonLSchembri.

By joining my email list, you will be among the first to know about upcoming events, products, services, additional tools, and tips that you won't get anywhere else.

In addition, I want to welcome you into a community of people who share the same challenges and want to journey towards mutual success and never return!

With sincere thanks and gratitude,

Jason L Schembri
The Weight Management Guy

About the Author

Born and raised in Melbourne, Australia, Jason L Schembri moved to Canada at the turn of the century and earned a professional designation in financial management. However, his passion for writing was always lurking beneath the surface. This was perhaps largely due to his mother being a school librarian during his childhood, and so it was, fortuitously, that Jason spent much of his childhood time being "day-cared" by a library and surrounded by the musty smell and loitering mysteries of a treasure chest of literary works.

Jason's education and career have not been in nutrition, dietary discipline, or personal training.

Jason, to put it simply, is an accountant. A long-spanning career in executive financial management (20+ years), supported by the appropriate professional designations. Jason is an expert at the analysis of numbers. He realized that drilling down into the numbers to discover and address root causes was also true of the human condition.

The author's rollercoaster struggle with weight management led to a great deal of scientific research, self-discovery, and extensive networking that all culminated in the development of tools and strategies that led to lasting success. This was achieved using the same principles that applied equally well to financial management, which in essence is also about the study of people's behaviors.

During his first few years in Canada, Jason gained about 120 pounds. The journey to losing this weight and the lessons learned along the way were shaped by the combination of Jason's upbringing, education, and professional experience.

Jason lived this journey and knew these struggles intimately, just as you do.

Jason's successful journey in weight loss was often marred by relapse after relapse until, over the course of about two decades, long-lasting success was finally achieved.

The writing of this book, spanning about 10 years, is something that Jason lives and breathes in his everyday life and is now the foundation of his passion and ministry in helping others achieve their success without having to go through the same lengthy struggles that he has faced.

Jason continues to live in Canada, where he shares the tools and strategies of his writing through coaching and speaking, striving to help as many people as he can by sharing his stories and experiences.

Through reading and learning, trying and failing, and finally succeeding, please join Jason in sharing the tools and strategies so that you, too, can keep it off and never go back.

Made in the USA
Monee, IL
11 August 2025

23102205R00066